This book belongs to

Age

Favourite player

Prediction of Ipswich Town's final position this season

Prediction of EFL Sky Bet Championship winners this season

Prediction of FA Cup winners this season

Prediction of EFL Cup winners this season

Prediction of teams to be relegated
from the EFL Sky Bet Championship this season:

22nd

23rd

24th

Written by twocan

Contributors: Lee Hyde,
Rob Mason & Peter Rogers

A TWOCAN PUBLICATION

©2016. Published by twocan under licence from Ipswich Town FC.

ISBN 978-1-909872-83-7

PICTURE CREDITS

£7.99

CONTENTS

THE TEAM

2016/17

Dean GERKEN 01

Position: Goalkeeper **Nationality:** English **DOB:** 22.05.85

Gerken is under contract until the end of the season. He will again battle it out with Bialkowski for the number one spot this term, both he and the Pole played over 20 matches each last term.

SQUAD 2016/17

Jonas KNUDSEN 03

Position: Defender **Nationality:** Danish **DOB:** 16.09.92

Knudsen joined the Blues on a three-year deal last summer, keeping him at the club until 2018. He scored his first goal for Town in a 1-1 draw with Fulham towards the end of the 2015/16 campaign.

Tommy
SMITH

05

Position: Defender **Nationality:** New Zealander **DOB:** 31.03.90

Smith progressed through the Academy ranks at the Club and is now a key player at the heart of defence. His displays last season didn't go unnoticed, as he came third in Town's Supporters' Player of the Year award.

Luke
CHAMBERS

04

Position: Defender **Nationality:** Irish **DOB:** 28.09.85

Chambers joined Ipswich back in 2012 on a free transfer after his contract at Nottingham Forest had expired. He impressed in his debut season and is now a well-established part of Town's defensive force.

Christophe
BERRA

06

Position: Defender **Nationality:** Scottish **DOB:** 31.01.85

A Scotland international, Berra joined The Blues on an initial two-year contract in 2013, although he is now under contract until the end of the 2016/17 season. He has firmly established himself as a regular in defence.

9

Teddy
BISHOP

 '07

Position: Midfielder **Nationality:** English **DOB:** 15.07.96

Bishop had an injury-hit 2015/16 and made his first appearance against Charlton in April. The tenacious midfielder will be hoping to push on further and cement his place in the squad again this term.

Cole
SKUSE

'08

Position: Midfielder **Nationality:** English **DOB:** 29.03.86

Skuse joined Ipswich Town in 2013 and extended his deal in 2015, keeping him at Portman Road until at least 2018. He won the 2014/15 Goal of the Season for his screamer in a 3-1 win over Cardiff at home.

Leon
BEST

'09

Position: Striker **Nationality:** Irish **DOB:** 19.09.86

Best joined Ipswich this August and brings a wealth of experience to the side having spent time at a number of clubs as well as representing the Republic of Ireland at U17, U19, U21 and at senior level.

David
McGOLDRICK | 10

Position: Striker **Nationality:** Irish **DOB:** 29.11.87

McGoldrick completed a permanent move to Town in 2013 after being on loan from Nottingham Forest. Last term he scored five goals and set up a further five, in all competitions, despite suffering a lengthy injury.

Brett
PITMAN | 11

Position: Striker **Nationality:** Jersey **DOB:** 31.01.88

After signing a three-year deal last summer, the 2015/16 season was Pitman's first at Portman Road and he finished as Ipswich Town's top scorer in all competitions with 11 strikes.

Paul
DIGBY | 14

Position: Defender **Nationality:** English **DOB:** 02.02.95

'Diggers' completed a permanent move to Ipswich this summer after a spell on loan. He has represented England in a range of different age groups and has trained with the first-team on occasion.

Luke
VARNEY | 12

Position: Striker **Nationality:** English **DOB:** 28.09.82

Varney initially joined Town on loan from Blackburn Rovers, before completing a permanent switch in December 2015. He quickly established himself as a popular figure with both the players and the fans after a number of wholehearted displays.

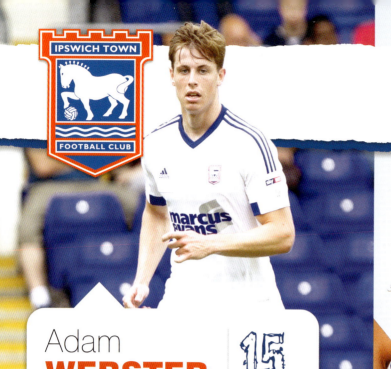

Adam WEBSTER 15

Position: Defender **Nationality:** English **DOB:** 05.01.95

Webster joined Town this summer from League Two side Portsmouth. His versatility has been highlighted by Mick McCarthy as an important part of his game as he is capable of playing at either centre-back or right-back.

Giles COKE 16

Position: Midfielder **Nationality:** English **DOB:** 03.06.86

Londoner Giles Coke, joined The Blues in the summer of 2015 after impressing whilst on trial. He adds a wealth of Championship experience to the squad having featured for a number of other clubs.

Kevin BRU 17

Position: Midfielder **Nationality:** Mauritian **DOB:** 12.12.88

Bru joined Ipswich Town in July 2014 after leaving Bulgarian side, Levski Sofia. He impressed last season and has become an important part of the squad owing to his range of passing and technique.

Grant WARD 18

Position: Midfielder **Nationality:** English **DOB:** 05.12.94

Ward joined Town from Tottenham this summer. He made an instant impact on his debut in the season opener against Barnsley and scored within 39 seconds before adding a further two goals to complete a hat-trick.

Luke
HYAM
19

Position: Midfielder **Nationality:** English **DOB:** 24.10.91

Hyam came through the Academy ranks at Portman Road and recently signed a new two-year contract, extending his Ipswich Town stay until 2018. He adds energy and tenacity to the Blues midfield.

Freddie
SEARS
20

Position: Striker **Nationality:** English **DOB:** 27.11.89

Sears signed for Town in January 2015 from Colchester United. He boasts impressive pace and versatility and notched four goals in his first six games last season.

Jonny
WILLIAMS
21

Position: Midfielder **Nationality:** Welsh **DOB:** 09.10.93

Williams recently returned to Town for his fourth loan spell from Crystal Palace. He penned a deal until the end of the season as he looks to build on impressive displays at the Euros with Wales.

Andre DOZZELL

Position: Midfielder **Nationality:** English **DOB:** 02.03.99

Dozzell is a product of the Blues' academy and the son of former Town star, Jason. He joined the Blues at just nine years old and has progressed right through the youth ranks into first-team contention.

Jonathan DOUGLAS

Position: Midfielder **Nationality:** Irish **DOB:** 22.11.81

Douglas signed for Town last summer. He has been capped eight times by the Republic of Ireland and made his Blues debut against former side Brentford, on the opening day of the 2015/16 season.

James BLANCHFIELD

Position: Midfielder **Nationality:** English **DOB:** 25.10.97

Blanchfield penned a one-year pro contract in July 2016 having progressed through the ITFC academy. He travelled with the first team for the match at Huddersfield in February 2016 and is a regular in Town's U21/U23 team.

Shane McLOUGHLIN

Position: Striker **Nationality:** Irish **DOB:** 01.03.97

McLoughlin has worked his way through the ranks at Town and is now challenging the first-team. He made a number of appearances during the 2016/17 pre-season and will hope to break through this term.

Adam McDONNELL 26

Position: Midfielder **Nationality:** Irish **DOB:** 14.05.97

McDonnell joined Town from Shelbourne in 2014. He is highly regarded at Town and has progressed through to the first-team, after having to wait a whole year to play competitive football, due to FIFA regulations.

Tom LAWRENCE 27

Position: Striker **Nationality:** Welsh **DOB:** 13.01.94

Lawrence joined the Blues this August on loan from Leicester City until the end of the season. He has represented Wales at U17, U19, U21 levels as well as making four appearances so far at senior level.

Conor GRANT 28

Position: Midfielder **Nationality:** English **DOB:** 18.04.95

A left-sided midfielder, Grant joined Town on a season-long loan from Everton this summer. It is his third loan spell having already spent time with Doncaster Rovers and Motherwell in recent years.

Josh EMMANUEL 29

Position: Defender **Nationality:** English **DOB:** 18.08.97

A strong defender, Emmanuel came through the academy ranks with the Blues and is highly regarded as one for the future. He made his first-team debut in 2015/16's opening day draw with Brentford.

Myles
KENLOCK

30

Position: Defender **Nationality:** English **DOB:** 29.11.96

Left-back Kenlock joined in 2014 as a scholar following trials at several clubs with some of those in the Premier League. He has impressed Mick McCarthy and made his full debut last season in the Capital One Cup win over Stevenage.

Kundai
BENYU

31

Position: Midfielder **Nationality:** English **DOB:** 12.12.97

Benyu is a central midfielder, academy graduate, who signed a first professional deal with the Club in February 2015, taking his stay with Town up until 2017.

Bartosz
BIALKOWSKI

33

Position: Goalkeeper **Nationality:** Polish **DOB:** 06.07.87

A towering Polish 'keeper, Bialkowski joined the Blues from Notts County in 2014. He won the Supporters' and the Players' Player of the Year award for his impressive form during the 2015/16 season.

Joe
ROBINSON

34

Position: Defender **Nationality:** English **DOB:** 10.08.96

Town defender Robinson has captained both the U18's and U21's teams. Joe has recently signed on loan for Boston United FC with the aim of gaining valuable first-team football experience.

Michael
CROWE

38

Position: Goalkeeper **Nationality:** Welsh **DOB:** 13.11.95

A young goalkeeper, Crowe is Town's number three stopper. He has impressed since arriving at Portman Road and has worked closely with first-team goalkeeping coach, Malcolm Webster.

Jacob
MARSDEN

Position: Goalkeeper **Nationality:** English **DOB:** 14.10.96

Marsden is an academy graduate who recently signed his first professional contract at Portman Road. Jacob is highly rated at Playford Road and has made a number of appearances for Town's U21/U23 team.

George
FOWLER

Position: Defender **Nationality:** English **DOB:** 20.12.97

Defender George recently signed his first professional deal with Town having progressed through the academy as a scholar. Fowler represented the U18's team at only 14 years old.

Monty
PATTERSON

Position: Striker **Nationality:** New Zealander **DOB:** 09.12.96

Patterson signed his first pro deal with Ipswich in July 2016 having been part of the Development squad. He was called up to the New Zealand national team for the 2016 OFC Nations Cup this summer and made his senior debut.

IPSWICH TOWN FOOTBALL CLUB

BrettPitman

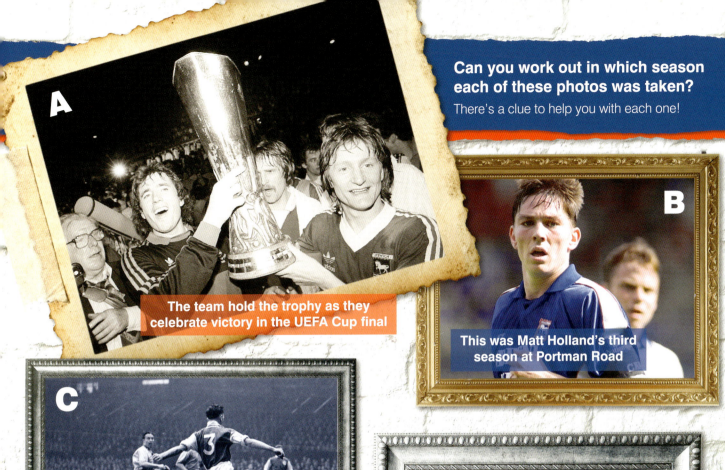

A

The team hold the trophy as they celebrate victory in the UEFA Cup final

Can you work out in which season each of these photos was taken?

There's a clue to help you with each one!

B

This was Matt Holland's third season at Portman Road

C

Action from a derby day win, Ipswich finished top of Division Three South this season

D

This campaign saw Christophe Berra named Player of the season

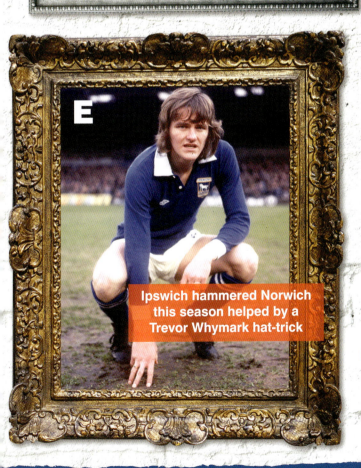

E

Ipswich hammered Norwich this season helped by a Trevor Whymark hat-trick

spot the **Season**

ANSWERS ON PAGE 62

19

There are five members of Team GB hidden in the crowd.
Can you find them all?

ANSWERS ON PAGE 62

Professional footballers at top level can run around 12 kilometres per game.

Quite often, they might have to play two matches within three or four days of each other and over the course of a season, regular players could play in the region of 50 games!

That would be a lot if they were simply running as a long distance runner does. In football though, that running is done with a mixture of short sprints from a standing start and runs of various lengths at differing intensities. On top of this, there is a lot of twisting and turning, often while someone is trying to pull the player back or even kick them.

If they can cope with this, there is then the consideration that once the footballer has the ball, they have to use it, either with a telling pass or a shot on goal, while the opposition do all they can to stop them. Added to this is the fact that the thousands of fans watching in the stadium and the millions viewing on TV are only too ready to criticise them if they do not get it right.

To cope with all this, players have to be supremely fit so they have the stamina to last 90 minutes on a regular basis, and have the competitive edge to deal with opponents trying to stop them. Players also have to be careful to eat and drink the right things, get the right amount of sleep and keep themselves in tip-top shape.

In the summer when players return from a few weeks off, they do a lot of physical training to get themselves ready for the big kick-off. Once a few games have been played and they have, what players call, 'match-fitness', their aim is to maintain that fitness, but not over-do things.

Most players will train for two or three hours most days and do additional work in the gym, as well as perhaps doing pilates or yoga to help look after their bodies. Cycling and swimming can be useful too, but so is knowing when to simply rest, because the Championship season is a long and gruelling campaign.

PRE-SEASON TRAINING

23

1

Draw back your foot as if you are going to kick the ball

2

Instead of following through, stop your foot over the ball ...

...and push it back behind your other leg while starting to turn your body.

3

Finish turning through 180° and head in the opposite direction.

4

Your unsuspecting opponent will be left standing wondering what just happened!

5

Johan Cruyff debuted his signature dummy at the 1974 FIFA World Cup. The trick is a brilliant manoeuvre to fool your opponent and change direction.

Luke**Chambers**

IPSWICH TOWN FOOTBALL CLUB

Here is the first half of our Championship A-Z. The answer to each clue begins with the corresponding letter of the alphabet.

See how much you really know!

A-Z OF

A — Newcastle were relegated to the Championship last season after finishing 18th, but this club was bottom of the table

B — The insects present on Brentford's club crest

C — Manager of Burton Albion when they were promoted from League One last season

D — Preston North End play their home games here

E — Wolves midfielder who was in Wales' squad for Euro 2016

F — Name of Brighton's stadium before it was sponsored by AMEX

G — Reading's top appearance maker last season

See how much
you really know!

I Derby play their home games here

H Blackburn's player of the 2015/16 season

Leeds United's kit manufacturer

J Wigan's Finnish goalie who helped them reach promotion last season

K

L Huddersfield played their home games here before the John Smith's Stadium

M The scorer of Birmingham's winning goal when they won the League Cup in 2011

Captain of Ipswich when they won the FA Cup and UEFA Cup, Mills also captained England at the 1982 World Cup. Town's record appearance maker with 561 league appearances, he later moved into management.

PAUL COOPER

Brilliant penalty saver who in 1978 and 1981 won the FA Cup and UEFA Cup with Ipswich for whom he made 447 league appearances.

GEORGE BURLEY

Classy Scotland international who played at the 1982 World Cup. An FA Cup winner, he was unlucky to miss the UEFA Cup final through injury. He went on to manage Ipswich from 1994 to 2002.

MICK MILLS

TERRY BUTCHER

Inspirational centre-back who played for England at three World Cups. Capped 77 times, Terry won 45 of them while with Ipswich. He won the UEFA Cup while at Portman Road and further trophies in Scotland with Rangers before becoming a manager.

DREAM

Despite an injury riddled career, Beattie was a magnificent defender. Player of the Year in consecutive campaigns Kevin was also the PFA Young Player of the Year in 1973/74. A Cup winner in 1978, he was an England international.

KEVIN BEATTIE

FRANS THIJSSEN

There's no substitute for class and Frans was Footballer of the Year when Ipswich won the UEFA Cup in 1981, having been Ipswich's Player of the Year a season earlier.

PAUL MARINER

In tandem with fellow Dutchman Thijssen, Muhren was magic. He won European trophies with Ipswich and Ajax and helped the Netherlands to become European champions in 1988. He was also Player of the Year at Ipswich in 1978/79.

ARNOLD MUHREN

JOHN WARK

Player of the Year a record four times, Wark is also the record scorer in derbies against Norwich. He won the FA Youth Cup, FA Cup and UEFA Cup while at Portman Road where in 1981 he was the PFA Player of the Year.

RAY CRAWFORD

England international who scored 204 league goals in 320 games. This included 40 as the second division was won in 1960 and 33 as the league title was lifted a year later, with Ray the country's joint top scorer.

CLIVE WOODS

Man of the Match when the FA Cup was won in 1978. Five years earlier winger Woods won the Texaco Cup with Ipswich. He was at Town from 1969 to 1980.

Mariner was an England centre forward who scored 96 top flight goals in 260 league games at Ipswich. While with Town he also won the FA Cup and UEFA Cup.

29

08

ColeSkuse

ON THE ROAD

Can you figure out where every team in the Championship plays their home games? Fill in the missing words and find all the grounds in the grid!

```
S R F C A R R O W R O A D S L N A L F S J D
E A T O A K W E L L S T A D I U M U K V O F
Y S K W S R I A E K O W O N T F E X B A H G
Q I F M V M D R S J G L D S A W X C T X N I
W S K U I U L I B H E S N J O M S I S D S P
N K G I L I E C F S T B H O U C T T M A M M
A E R D L D M V Y F A O D G Y L A Y U O I U
P L I A A A R G L D C P N Y E N D G I R T I
O A F T P T U J R O A I S G D Y I R D D H D
R D F S A S V D V R F J T R A H U O A N S A
T P I W R I E C K O B T E Y C T M U T A S T
M E N D K K Z M T M D W U G S K E N S L T S
A E P L D S B P A S S O T S F T B D O L A I
N D A R Q J F H N J I M Y Z R U A O R E D L
R C R A V E N C O T T A G E D O E D P N I L
O U K E H D P V J F M S P C I P A R I G U E
A E S S E A L N E W Y O R K S T A D I U M R
D N W T A M U I D A T S X U E N I L O M M I
H I L L S B O R O U G H Q O H G S G E A T P
```

Aston Villa	_ _ _ _ _ Park	Cardiff	_ _ _ _ _ _ _ City Stadium	Nottm Forest	City _ _ _ _ _ _
Barnsley	_ _ _ _ _ _ _ Stadium	Derby	_ _ _ _ Stadium	Preston	_ _ _ _ _ _ _
Birmingham	St _ _ _ _ _ _ _	Fulham	Craven _ _ _ _ _ _ _	QPR	_ _ _ _ _ _ Road
Blackburn	_ _ _ _ _ Park	Huddersfield	John _ _ _ _ _ _ Stadium	Reading	_ _ _ _ _ _ _ _ Stadium
Brentford	Griffin _ _ _ _	Ipswich	_ _ _ _ _ _ _ Road	Rotherham	AESSEAL _ _ _ _ _ _ Stadium
Brighton	_ _ _ _ Stadium	Leeds	Elland _ _ _ _	Sheff Wed	_ _ _ _ _ _ _ _ _ _ _
Bristol City	_ _ _ _ _ _ Gate	Newcastle	St _ _ _ _ _ Park	Wigan	DW _ _ _ _ _ _ _
Burton	_ _ _ _ _ _ _ Stadium	Norwich	_ _ _ _ _ _ Road	Wolves	_ _ _ _ _ _ _ _ Stadium

ANSWERS ON PAGE 62

DANGER MEN

ASTON VILLA
ROSS McCORMACK

One of the costliest strikers in the Championship, Scotland international McCormack cost Fulham £11m in 2014 with the Cottagers making a profit of £1m when Villa bought the Glasgow born hot-shot at the start of this season. The 30-year-old has scored over 150 goals in his career and is a man who creates many more.

BARNSLEY
TOM BRADSHAW

Having scored 20 goals in each of the last two seasons Bradshaw was disappointed to lose to Barnsley in last season's League One Play-Offs for Walsall - but then signed for the Tykes. Having scored a League Cup hat-trick against Championship side Forest last season, the Wales international got his first goal in this season's Championship in a South Yorkshire derby against Rotherham at the end of August.

BIRMINGHAM CITY
CLAYTON DONALDSON

Jamaican international Donaldson is a great spearhead for The Blues. Good in the air, determined and mobile he has scored over 40 goals for three different clubs and could equal that achievement with a good season for Birmingham for whom he has bagged 27 in the past two seasons.

BLACKBURN ROVERS
DANNY GRAHAM

A well-travelled target man, Danny Graham impressed on loan for Rovers last season before signing for them in the summer. With well over 100 goals in his career, Graham's best haul was 27 with Watford in 2010/11 - 24 of those were in the Championship in what was his last full season spent at this level.

BRENTFORD
SCOTT HOGAN

Hogan could be a hero for the Bees this season and be their secret weapon. Having played for six non-league clubs he was given a chance by Rochdale who he had played for at Academy level. Hogan quickly made up for lost time, a debut goal being Sky TV's 'Goal of the Day'. It was the first of 19 he got that season as he fired Rochdale to promotion, was voted Player of the Year and into the PFA League Two team. Badly injured soon after a move to Brentford, he returned with seven goals in seven games late last season.

BRIGHTON & HOVE ALBION
TOMER HEMED

The 29-year-old Israel international is a big part of Brighton's promotion hopes. Having played in Spain as well as his home country, Hemed scored 16 goals in 40 games in his first season in English football last season and Chris Hughton will look to bring the best out of him once again this time round.

Watch out for these dangermen when the Blues meet their Championship rivals...

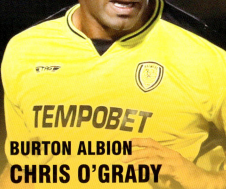

BRISTOL CITY
TAMMY ABRAHAM

With 74 goals in 98 games for Chelsea at youth level the question is can England U20 speed merchant Abraham do it at first team level? Given a Chelsea debut against Liverpool last season, Abraham found the net four times in his first six outings on loan to Bristol City. If Tammy keeps it up he could be this season's 'Rockin' Robin'.

BURTON ALBION
CHRIS O'GRADY

On loan from Brighton, O'Grady has had so many loans he might think he's a high street bank, his current stint with Burton being his tenth. On loan from Brighton, Chris started this season three goals short of a century. Not always prolific, he can be - netting 15 in 2013/14 - but he's always a handful and is key to Burton doing well this season following last year's promotion.

CARDIFF CITY
RICKIE LAMBERT

Approaching 250 career goals - over 100 of them for one club (Southampton) - Rickie Lambert is a lethal finisher. The sheer number of his goals earned him an England debut in 2013 and he scored with his first touch, heading home against Scotland. Now 32, Lambert isn't the quickest, but his game has never been based on pace.

DERBY COUNTY
MATEJ VYDRA

The Rams paid a reported £8m to snap up the 24-year-old Czech Republic hitman who was the Championship Player of the Year in 2013 after netting 20 goals in 41 games for Watford. A nippy goal-poacher Vydra played in his home country as well as Italy and Belgium before coming into English football where he has also played for WBA and Reading.

FULHAM
CHRIS MARTIN

Chris Martin might feel destiny would bring him to Fulham who he joined on a season-long loan from Derby just as the transfer window closed. Having played for England at U19 level he decided to play for Scotland and made his international debut in 2014 against Nigeria…at Fulham's Craven Cottage! Great in the air, Martin is one of the best strikers in the league.

HUDDERSFIELD TOWN
NAHKI WELLS

Having hit 17 goals last season, Wells will hope to maintain that level of consistency for the Terriers. Nahki came to the fore at nearby Bradford City for whom he played in the League Cup final in 2013 after scoring in the semi-final against Aston Villa. Pacey, persistent and with the ability to finish, Wells is always a tough customer.

Watch out for these dangermen when the Blues meet their Championship rivals...

IPSWICH TOWN
BRETT PITMAN

A consistent goal-scorer who notched 11 goals for the Tractor Boys last season and 14 the year before as part of Bournemouth's title-winning team. Following Ipswich's sale of Daryl Murphy to Newcastle at the start of the season, the Club's need for Pitman to be among the goals will be even more important this time round.

LEEDS UNITED
CHRIS WOOD

Twice a promotion winner to the Premier League, Leeds will hope Wood can complete a notable hat-trick at Elland Road. A New Zealand international who played at the World Cup finals in 2010, Chris won promotion to the Championship with Brighton and into the top flight with both West Brom and Leicester.

NEWCASTLE UNITED
DWIGHT GAYLE

Lift off for the man whose first club was Stansted came when Newcastle United paid £10m to bring the Londoner from Crystal Palace. Gayle's first ever Premier League goal came against Newcastle in his Palace days and he made a good start at firing the Magpies back towards the top flight with four goals in his first four games for Rafa Benitez's side.

NORWICH CITY
SERGI CANOS

A former Barcelona youth player, Sergi played once for Liverpool before spending last season on loan to Brentford where he scored seven and made five goals as a winger. Still a teenager the Spain U19 international cost the Canaries £2.5m in the summer to bring him from Anfield and he could well be a potent weapon whenever he is on the ball for City.

NOTTINGHAM FOREST
BRITT ASSOMBALONGA

23 goals in 43 games for Peterborough in 2013/14 signalled Assombalonga's goal threat, Posh having already recognised that when making the Watford Academy product their record signing. A bad injury cost Britt 14 months of his career having also broken Forest's transfer record but with 19 goals in his first 36 games he remains one of the hottest properties in the Championship.

PRESTON NORTH END
DANIEL JOHNSON

Given a new contract early this season, Johnson is Preston's midfield creator and offers a goal threat coming in from the left. Having been schooled in the youth systems at Palace and Villa the Jamaican came to Preston in January 2015, helped North End to promotion and is at the heart of much of their best attacking play.

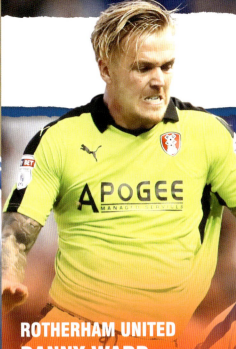

QUEENS PARK RANGERS
TJARONN CHERY

Hoops' Player of the Year last season, Tjaronn scored three goals in the first four games of this season, his first campaign in English football. Now 28, Chery was called into an international squad for Holland in May 2015 after scoring 15 times in his last season with Groningen.

READING
YANN KERMORGANT

The aerial ability of the veteran French striker can be a key asset for Jaap Stam's side. Kermorgant helped Bournemouth to the Championship title in 2015 when he scored 17 goals in all competitions and was nominated for the Championship goal of the season for one of his trademark bicycle kicks.

ROTHERHAM UNITED
DANNY WARD

Rotherham will fight hard to stay up this year with Danny Ward a key man for the Millers. He scored on the opening day of the season against Wolves and soon followed that up with a vital winner against Brentford. On his day he can be lethal, as he showed with a Championship hat-trick away to Watford in May 2014 in his Huddersfield days. 25 just before Christmas, Ward's form is likely to be key to Rotherham's progress.

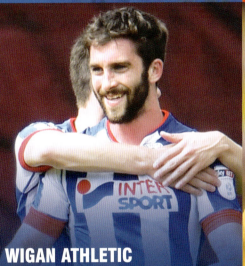

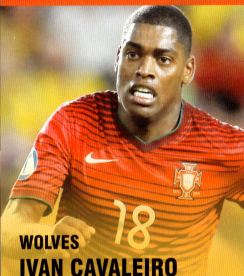

SHEFFIELD WEDNESDAY
STEVEN FLETCHER

Scotland international striker Fletcher spent the latter part of last season in France with Marseille - making his debut against PSG when he came on for Michy Batshuayi who Chelsea have since paid mega-money for. One of the best headers of the ball in the game, the former Hibs, Burnley, Wolves and Sunderland man can be deadly on any day of the week.

WIGAN ATHLETIC
WILL GRIGG

The song 'Will Grigg's on Fire' reached the iTunes top 10 last season as the Northern Ireland international fired in 28 goals on top of the 22 he'd struck the season before. Showing no signs that his form had been dampened the 25-year-old began with a bang this term, scoring four times in his first five games. If he's heading for your defence dial 999 in case of emergency.

WOLVES
IVAN CAVALEIRO

As a former goalie, Wolves boss Walter Zenga knows a dangerman when he sees one and broke Wanderers' club record to bring in Portugal international Cavaleiro for a reported £7m. The 23-year-old can play on the wing or up front and has played Champions League football for Benfica and Monaco. As an U21 international he hit a hat-trick on his debut against Switzerland in 2013.

SKILLS: Rainbow Kick

1
Start off with your feet on either side of the ball

2
Use one foot to roll the ball up your other leg

3
Make sure to roll the ball hard enough to give it some air

4
When the ball is in the air strike it with your heel

5
...and flick it over your head!

Brazilian star striker, Neymar, is well known for his use of the rainbow kick on the pitch and regularly fools his opposition. The trick is an impressive show of skill which takes practise, practise practise!

TIP: Lean forward as you're doing the trick, this helps create space between you and the ball so you can strike it more easily.

Jonas Knudsen

03

IPSWICH TOWN FOOTBALL CLUB

Can you figure out the identity of these Ipswich stars?

A

B

E

Who are yer?

ANSWERS ON PAGE 62

Andre Dozzell is an attacking midfielder who burst into the Ipswich Town FC first-team squad, aged just 16, with a headed goal on his senior debut at Sheffield Wednesday in April 2016. This achievement matched his father, Jason Dozzell's effort, of scoring on his professional debut, also aged 16 for Town in 1984.

Andre is an exciting player and a product of the Ipswich Town youth academy. Having had an outstanding season with the academy and U21 team, resulting in a number of appearances in the first-team squad, Andre was awarded with the club's Academy Player of the Year award at the 2015/16 awards dinner. It capped a wonderful season for Andre having also played for and captained the England U17 team on several occasions.

Following in his father's footsteps, Andre is quickly becoming a fan's favourite at Portman Road. 2016/17 looks to be the season where Andre will breakthrough into the first-team squad on a regular basis and make his name within the team. Andre will wear the squad number 23 for the new season - be sure to watch out for him in the EFL Sky Bet Championship!

wonderkid

Town's Mauritian midfielder Kevin Bru was the standout choice as the 2015/16 Goal of the Season.

As with the previous season's winner (Cole Skuse), this goal was of the highest calibre, a long range effort from midfield giving the opposition goalkeeper no chance.

Ipswich Town were taking on Bolton Wanderers at the Macron stadium on Tuesday, 8th March 2016, in front of 12,681 fans. The game burst into life after 24 minutes when a cross from the left touchline was flicked on by Luke Chambers, brought down by Christophe Berra and laid back into the path of the dynamic Town midfielder. Bru hit a curling, dipping strike from 25 yards which flew over the top of Paul Rachubka in the Bolton goal and crashed into the net off the underside of the crossbar.

Town doubled their advantage in the 72nd minute with Christophe Berra heading the Blues into a commanding 2-0 lead. Unfortunately Ipswich couldn't hold onto the lead and were pegged back firstly through a Laurie Wilson half-volley within 90 seconds of Berra's goal, then with almost the last kick of the game as Stephen Dobbie converted a 97th minute penalty. The match finished 2-2 with Ipswich remaining in 7th place in the division.

GOAL OF THE SEASON

Can you work out in which season each of these photos was taken?
There's a clue to help you with each one!

spot the season

A

All-time top appearance maker Mick Mills during his last season at the club

B

John Lyall guided Ipswich to the Division Two Championship and promotion this season

C

A 2-1 derby day victory at Portman Road, Kuqi celebrates after Norwich City's Alex Pearce scores an own goal!

D

First Division Champions this season

E

The FA Cup winning team!

ANSWERS ON PAGE 62

Here is the second half of our Championship A-Z.

The answer to each clue begins with the corresponding letter of the alphabet.

A-Z OF THE

N QPR manager Jimmy Floyd Hasselbaink played for this national team

O He scored the winning goal when Ipswich won the FA Cup in 1978

P Fulham captain and former England international

One of Brentford's main rivals

Q

R Aston Villa's number four defender

S The team Norwich beat in the final of the League Cup in 1985

See how much you really know!

T

rnsley's ckname

U

The animal on Bristol City's crest

V

Czech striker who signed for Derby this August

W

Sheffield Wednesday's goalie

X

Newcastle manager, Rafa Benitez, bought and sold this Spanish midfielder while at Liverpool

Y

Young Rotherham forward

Z

Danish striker who signed for Cardiff this summer

DESIGN YOUR OWN FOOTIE BOOTS

Grant Ward

WHAT BALL?

A

B

DARYL MURPHY

There's very little to put a smile on a striker's face more than scoring a hat-trick in a winning performance.

Take a look back at three special Blues trebles...

HAT-TRICK

Rotherham United 2 Ipswich Town 5

Saturday 7 November 2015

Town's Republic of Ireland striker Daryl Murphy netted a memorable hat-trick in the highly entertaining 5-2 victory over Rotherham United at the New York Stadium last season.

Murphy's treble saw him become the first Town player to hit a hat-trick since Connor Wickham helped himself to a treble in the 6-0 victory away to Doncaster Rovers in February 2011.

Town were already two goals to the good against the Millers thanks to strikes from Brett Pitman and Jonathan Douglas when Murphy got in on the act. The powerful frontman grabbed his first of the afternoon two minutes before the break to give Mick McCarthy's men a three-goal cushion at the break.

Murphy then started the second-half in similar vein by making it 4-0 three minutes after the re-start. The home side did pull two goals back before Murphy completed his hat-trick on 72 minutes.

Ipswich Town 6-0 Manchester Utd

Saturday 1 March 1980

A close First Division match was expected to be on the cards when second placed Manchester United visited Portman Road to take on third placed Town in 1979/80. However, Town striker Paul Mariner and his teammates had clearly not read the script! From the moment Alan Brazil opened the scoring the game was anything but a close contest.

Despite this being an exceptional all-round team performance, Mariner was the man who grabbed the headlines with his hat-trick heroics. He netted his first and Town's second goal of the game before slamming home his second to make it 3-0 after just 27 minutes. A second goal for Brazil came after the break and Frans Thijssen was also on target before Mariner completed his treble and sealed a 6-0 win.

This was a memorable afternoon at Portman Road and a game that also saw United 'keeper Gary Bailey amazingly save three Ipswich penalties! Certainly one to ask dad and grandad about!

ALEX MATHIE

HEROES

Ipswich Town 5-0 Norwich City

Saturday 21 February 1998

Scottish striker Alex Mathie wrote his name into Portman Road folklore with a devastating first-half hat-trick as Town thrashed local rivals Norwich City 5-0 in the East Anglian derby.

After suffering a 2-1 defeat at Carrow Road earlier in the season Town were chasing both a play-off place and local pride. Town went into this game in fine form while the Canaries struggled to name eleven fit men and always looked set for a hammering. It took Mathie just 64 seconds to begin the rout when he fired home in front of a delighted Churchman's.

Mathie doubled Town's lead on 27 minutes and completed his hat-trick just three minutes before the break to secure himself the match ball. He left the Portman Road pitch to a standing ovation at half-time with Town fans knowing both three points and local pride were secured.

Bobby Petta added Town's two further goals after the break on a memorable afternoon for the home fans inside Portman Road.

PAUL MARINER

Bartosz Bialkowski, Town's Polish goalkeeper, walked away with the Ipswich Town Supporters Club Player of the Season award for the 2015/16 season, ahead of Freddie Sears (2nd) and Tommy Smith (3rd) respectively.

Bialkowski also picked up the Junior Blues' Player of the Year, Players' Player of the Year and Corporate customers, Box holders and Sponsors Player of the Year awards.

The Polish goalkeeper had faced competition from Dean Gerken throughout the season. The latter picked up an injury in early 2016 giving 'Bart' his chance between the posts. After a string of impressive displays and consecutive Player of the Month awards, Bartosz became a real fan's favourite at Portman Road.

Originating from Braniewo, the 29-year-old, 6ft 4in keeper is a giant in the Town goal. His agility and shot-stopping has earned rave reviews from both fans and media alike. After making over 50 appearances for the Club, Bartosz has cemented his place as one of the top goalkeepers in England, outside of the Premier League.

His presence, ability and man of the match performances throughout both the 2014/15 and 2015/16 seasons have been the catalyst for Ipswich Town FC's rise up the Championship. There have been many occasions when Bartosz's contribution in matches has resulted in Town keeping a clean sheet and taking all three points on offer.

PLAYER OF THE YEAR

SKILLS: Maradona Spin

1 Start off by simply dribbling the ball

2 While moving in a forward motion, tap the ball with your leading foot...

3 ...and start turning your body in the opposite direction

4 As you're spinning, pull the ball back with your other foot while continuing to turn

5

6 Then keep moving forward!

Argentinian maestro, Maradona, is very well known for this move. It is brilliant for overcoming opponents and getting yourself into space, as while you are spinning you are putting your back to the defender and shielding the ball.

CLUB OR COUNTRY?

Can you work out which team each set of clues is pointing to... they could be Premier League, Championship or international.

1.

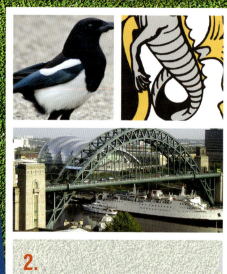

2.

3.

4.

5.

6.

7.

8.

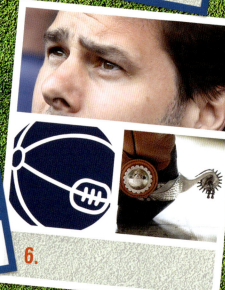

9.

David McGoldrick

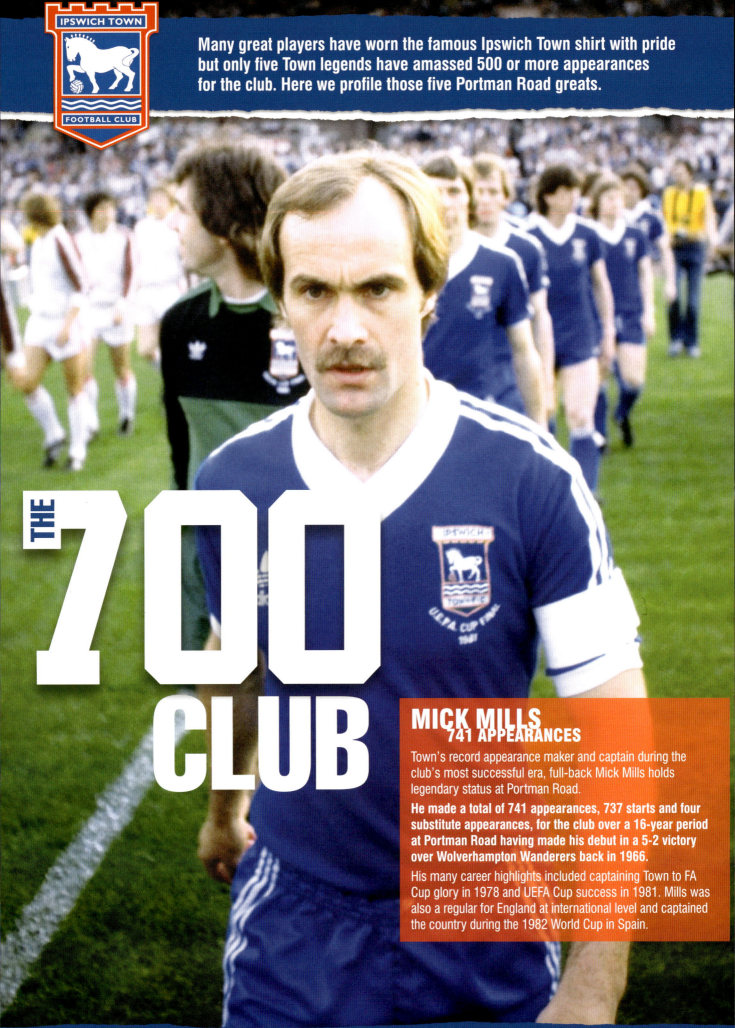

Many great players have worn the famous Ipswich Town shirt with pride but only five Town legends have amassed 500 or more appearances for the club. Here we profile those five Portman Road greats.

THE 700 CLUB

MICK MILLS
741 APPEARANCES

Town's record appearance maker and captain during the club's most successful era, full-back Mick Mills holds legendary status at Portman Road.

He made a total of 741 appearances, 737 starts and four substitute appearances, for the club over a 16-year period at Portman Road having made his debut in a 5-2 victory over Wolverhampton Wanderers back in 1966.

His many career highlights included captaining Town to FA Cup glory in 1978 and UEFA Cup success in 1981. Mills was also a regular for England at international level and captained the country during the 1982 World Cup in Spain.

THE 600 CLUB

JOHN WARK
678 APPEARANCES

Goalscoring midfielder John Wark amassed at total of 678 appearances for Town, 670 starts and eight substitute appearances, over three separate spells with the club.

Born in Glasgow, Wark suffered from home sickness when he first arrived in Suffolk but soon progressed through the youth and reserve ranks to become a star performer under Sir Bobby Robson.

A member of Town's 1978 FA Cup winning team, Wark's goals were the catalyst for the club's UEFA Cup triumph in 1981. He scored 14 goals in the competition including one in each leg of the final as Town overcame Dutch side AZ Alkmaar 5-4 on aggregate.

MICK STOCKWELL
608 APPEARANCES

Essex-born Micky Stockwell was part of a highly successful youth system at Portman Road put in place by Sir Bobby Robson.

The ever-reliable and hard-working midfielder made at total of 608 appearances in an Ipswich shirt - 555 starts and 53 substitute appearances. He also scored 44 goals for the club.

Stockwell played a vital role in Town's 1991/92 Second Division championship-winning campaign under John Lyall and he also featured regularly in the first Premier League season of 1992/93. He was granted a testimonial in 1994 and remained the mainstay of the Town side that attempted to win promotion back to the Premier League in the 1996/97 and 1997/98 campaigns. He ended his playing career with a spell at Colchester United.

THE 500 CLUB

PAUL COOPER
575 APPEARANCES

Former Town goalkeeper Paul Cooper was born in Staffordshire in 1953 and began his professional career with Birmingham City.

After 17 league matches for the St Andrew's club he joined Town in 1974 and proceeded to become a cult hero who played 575 times for the club. Cooper was an excellent all-round 'keeper with assured handling and great reflexes but it was his remarkable ability to save penalties that saw him become such a terrace hero. In the 1979/80 season he saved an incredible eight out of ten penalties.

A member of the 1978 FA Cup winning team and also a UEFA Cup winner in 1981, Cooper remains the Town 'keeper that all others will be judged against.

GEORGE BURLEY
500 APPEARANCES

The final member of this exclusive group, George Burley went on to enjoy both a highly successful managerial career at Portman Road after playing 500 times for the club between 1973 and 1985.

The first of Burley's 500 outings for Town came at Old Trafford in 1973 when he was handed the task of marking the legendary George Best! Burley went on to the make the right-back berth his own and was a member of 1978 FA Cup winning team but injury sadly ruled him out of Town's 1981 UEFA Cup success over AZ Alkmaar.

After later playing for Sunderland and Gillingham before returning north of the border to end his playing career, Burley became Town manager in November 1994. As boss he oversaw promotion to the Premier League in 2000 via the play-offs and then guided Town to fifth place in the Premier League in 2000/01.

The second half of the 2016/17 season certainly looks to be an exciting affair for all at Portman Road. We take a look at five key fixtures scheduled for the latter stages of the current campaign.

TUESDAY 31 JANUARY · PORTMAN ROAD
DERBY COUNTY

Town complete the busy month of January with a midweek fixture at home to Derby County on Tuesday 31 January.

The Rams reached the play-off semi-finals last season only to miss out on Wembley after suffering a defeat to eventual promotion winners Hull City. Now under the management of former Leicester City boss Nigel Pearson, an awful lot is expected of the Rams once again in 2016/17.

After both of last season's corresponding fixtures ended in 1-0 away wins it's difficult to predict anything other than yet another hard fought and tight affair when the two sides meet under the Portman Road floodlights.

SATURDAY 11 FEBRUARY · VILLA PARK
ASTON VILLA

The Tractor boys will head off to Villa Park for a league fixture for the first time in 16 years when they take on Roberto Di Matteo's Aston Villa on Saturday 11 February.

After suffering relegation from the Premier League for the first time in the club's history, the Midlands giants will be doing all they can to engineer a return to the top flight at the first time of asking. Di Matteo has assembled an experienced back room staff and has strengthened his playing squad over the summer most notably with the arrival of former Bournemouth captain Tommy Elphick.

This is sure to be a tough assignment for Town as they look to record victory on a ground they have not won at since a Chris Swailes' own goal sealed a 1-0 Town triumph in March 1994.

SATURDAY 18 FEBRUARY · PORTMAN ROAD
LEEDS UNITED

February has certainly presented Town with some attractive and challenging fixtures and none more so than the visit of Leeds United on Saturday the 18th.

Having appointed former Swansea City manager Garry Monk to the Elland Road hot-seat in the summer, there will be an increased level of expectancy surrounding Leeds United in 2016/17. Summer recruits include Swedish striker Marcus Antonsson and former England 'keeper Robert Green.

Last season saw Town record a memorable double over Leeds after a 1-0 win at Elland Road was followed up with a 2-1 Portman Road victory. Another six points off of this tough opponent would be most welcome in 2016/17.

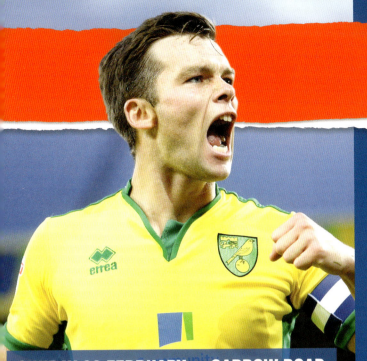

SUNDAY 26 FEBRUARY · CARROW ROAD
NORWICH CITY

Town will head into enemy territory for the return leg of the East Anglian Derby on Sunday 26 February when they come face-to-face with arch-rivals Norwich City at a packed Carrow Road.

Revenge will certainly be on Mick McCarthy's men's minds after suffering both a league loss and the painful blow of a play-off semi-final loss to the Canaries at Carrow Road in 2014/15.

Despite their relegation from the Premier League last season, Alex Neil's Norwich side are expected to be among the serious promotion contenders once again come the business end of the season.

MONDAY 17 APRIL · PORTMAN ROAD
NEWCASTLE UNITED

The Portman Road faithful will have to wait until the penultimate home game of the season to see promotion favourites Newcastle United make their eagerly-awaited visit to Suffolk.

Rafa Benitez's star-studded squad will provide the opposition at Portman Road on Easter Monday in a fixture most Town fans have already earmarked as a must-see fixture in the second half of the season.

With the late Sir Bobby Robson being in the hearts and minds of supporters of both clubs it's sure to be an emotional and entertaining Easter fixture here at Portman Road.

January 2017

Mon	02	QPR	A	3.00pm
Sat	**14**	**Blackburn**	**H**	**3.00pm**
Sat	21	Huddersfield	A	3.00pm
Sat	28	Preston North End	A	3.00pm
Tue	**31**	**Derby**	**H**	**7.45pm**

February 2017

Sat	**04**	**Reading**	**H**	**3.00pm**
Sat	11	Aston Villa	A	3.00pm
Tue	14	Brighton	A	7.45pm
Sat	**18**	**Leeds**	**H**	**3.00pm**
Sun	26	Norwich City	A	12 noon

March 2017

Sat	**04**	**Brentford**	**H**	**3.00pm**
Tue	**07**	**Wolves**	**H**	**7.45pm**
Sat	11	Barnsley	A	3.00pm
Sat	18	Cardiff	A	3.00pm

April 2017

Sat	**01**	**Birmingham**	**H**	**3.00pm**
Tue	**04**	**Wigan**	**H**	**7.45pm**
Sat	08	Fulham	A	3.00pm
Fri	14	Burton Albion	A	3.00pm
Mon	**17**	**Newcastle**	**H**	**3.00pm**
Sat	22	Rotherham	A	3.00pm
Sat	**29**	**Sheff Wed**	**H**	**3.00pm**

May 2017

Sun	07	Nottingham Forest	A	12 noon

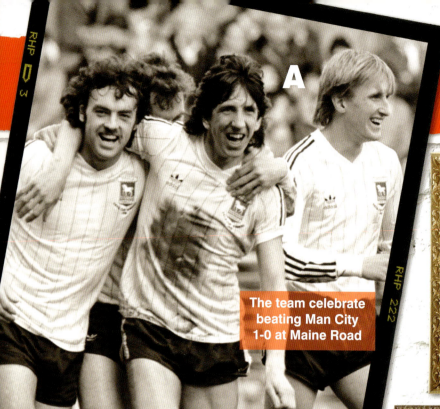

The team celebrate beating Man City 1-0 at Maine Road

Can you work out in which season each of these photos was taken?

There's a clue to help you with each one!

Ipswich did the double over Norwich this season, Dozzell scoring two in the 3-1 win at Portman Road

Ipswich finished third in the Championship this season, Shefki Kuqi was top scorer

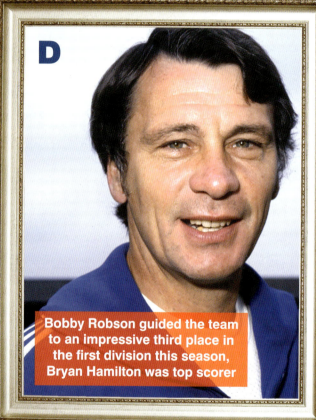

Bobby Robson guided the team to an impressive third place in the first division this season, Bryan Hamilton was top scorer

Connor Wickham became the youngest first team player this season at 16 years and 11 days

spot the Season

KevinBru

PREMIER LEAGUE

PREDICTION FOR PREMIER LEAGUE WINNERS:

Manchester Utd

YOUR PREDICTION:

PREDICTION FOR PREMIER LEAGUE RUNNERS-UP:

Chelsea

YOUR PREDICTION:

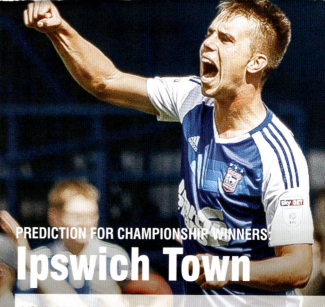

PREDICTION FOR CHAMPIONSHIP WINNERS:

Ipswich Town

YOUR PREDICTION:

PREDICTION FOR ALSO PROMOTED TO THE PREMIER LEAGUE:

Derby County & Brighton & HA

YOUR PREDICTION:

THE CHAMPIONSHIP

PREDICTIONS

THE FA CUP

PREDICTION FOR FA CUP WINNERS:
Crystal Palace

YOUR PREDICTION:

PREDICTION FOR FA CUP FINALISTS:
Liverpool

YOUR PREDICTION:

PREDICTION FOR LEAGUE CUP WINNERS:
Arsenal

YOUR PREDICTION:

PREDICTION FOR LEAGUE CUP FINALISTS:
Manchester City

YOUR PREDICTION:

THE LEAGUE CUP

ANSWERS

PAGE 19 · SPOT THE SEASON

a. 1980/81, b. 1999/2000, c. 1953/54, d. 2013/14, e. 1976/77.

PAGE 20 · FANTASTIC

Andy Murray, Jessica Ennis-Hill, Nicola Adams, Bradley Wiggins and Greg Rutherford.

PAGE 26 · A-Z OF THE CHAMPIONSHIP

a. Aston Villa, b. Bees, c. Nigel Clough, d. Deepdale, e. Dave Edwards, f. Falmer Stadium, g. Chris Gunter, h. Grant Hanley, i. iPro Stadium, j. Jussi Jaaskelainen, k. Kappa, l. Leeds Road, m. Obafemi Martins.

PAGE 31 · ON THE ROAD

Aston Villa - Villa Park, Barnsley - Oakwell Stadium, Birmingham - St Andrew's, Blackburn - Ewood Park, Brentford - Griffin Park, Brighton - AMEX Stadium, Bristol City - Ashton Gate, Burton - Pirelli Stadium, Cardiff - Cardiff City Stadium, Derby - iPro Stadium, Fulham - Craven Cottage, Huddersfield - John Smith's Stadium, Ipswich - Portman Road, Leeds - Elland Road, Newcastle - St James' Park, Norwich - Carrow Road, Nottm Forest - City Ground, Preston - Deepdale, QPR - Loftus Road, Reading - Madejski Stadium, Rotherham - AESSEAL New York Stadium, Sheff Wed - Hillsborough, Wigan - DW Stadium, Wolves - Molineux Stadium.

PAGE 38 · WHO ARE YER?

a. Luke Hyam, b. Luke Chambers, c. David McGoldrick, d. Adam Webster, e. Cole Skuse, f. Andre Dozzell, g. Tommy Smith.

PAGE 43 · SPOT THE SEASON

a. 1981/82, b. 1991/92, c. 2007/08, d. 1961/62, e. 1977/78.

PAGE 44
A-Z OF THE CHAMPIONSHIP

n. the Netherlands, o. Roger Osborne, p. Scott Parker, q. QPR, r. Micah Richards, s. Sunderland, t. the Tykes, u. Unicorn, v. Matej Vydra, w. Keiren Westwood, x. Xabi Alonso, y. Jerry Yates, z. Kenneth Zohore.

PAGE 48 · WHAT BALL?

Picture A - Ball 1, Picture B - Ball 2.

PAGE 52 · CLUB OR COUNTRY?

1. Hull City, 2. Newcastle United, 3. Spain, 4. Austria, 5. Wigan Athletic, 6. Tottenham Hotspur, 7. Iceland, 8. Arsenal, 9. Wolverhampton Wanderers.

PAGE 58 · SPOT THE SEASON

a. 1982/83, b. 1992/93, c. 2004/05, d. 1974/75, e. 2008/09.